Agnes Walsh

The Wind Has Robbed the Legs Off a Madwoman

poems

BREAKWATER
P.O. Box 2188, St. John's, NL, Canada, A1C 6E6
WWW.BREAKWATERBOOKS.COM

A CIP catalogue record for this book is available from Library and Archives Canada.

©2024 Agnes Walsh

Cover painting: *Drowning Woman*, oil on canvas, by Frank Barry

ISBN 9781778530166 (softcover)

We acknowledge the support of the Canada Council for the Arts. We acknowledge the financial support of the Government of Canada through the Department of Heritage and the Government of Newfoundland and Labrador through the Department of Tourism, Culture, Arts and Recreation for our publishing activities.

PRINTED AND BOUND IN CANADA.

 Canada Council for the Arts · Conseil des Arts du Canada Canadä · Newfoundland Labrador · Arts NL

Breakwater Books is committed to choosing papers and materials for our books that help to protect our environment. This book is printed on a recycled paper and other controlled sources that are certified by the Forest Stewardship Council®.

FSC
www.fsc.org

MIX
Paper from
responsible sources
FSC® C103567

for Marie-Annick

Contents

Seeing Nothing

Seeing nothing, even though
you are looking at what is there.
The long stretch of Cape road,
the caribou in a herd. You feel
the silence in their bodies,
watch their ears twitch
at the swirling snow.

They stare in a foreign tongue
that you almost understand.
The crows fly backwards
in the updraft of snow.

The car heater cocoons you,
lulling your body into a delta
of peace, of steamed windows.

The crack you make in the window
lets the outside in, tells you
this is the caribou's world.
You are only a thief in the night
stealing emptiness.

You Can Go Up from the Sand
and the Waves

and on every cliffside luminous lilies
made their escape through stones
—ALICE OSWALD

You can go up from the sand and the waves,
from the rocks folded into each other.
You can walk through thickets of tuckamore,
and there, in the hush of dense evergreen,
that lies so close to the earth,
there you can hear the sea.

But in here it is dulled. The gnarled trees have
gathered the sound: it has become a small ball
that you can round into your body, that you can
use to make you quiet. The scent of var,
of juniper berries, of that one wild violet,
can all be gathered without touching, without removing.

The tuckamore gives all this, holds it low.
Then it gives you shadows
that waver between light and dark.

And even sleep.
Even a dream.

Driving into the Waves

Driving into the waves of clouds,
the altocumulus, static as if frozen,
as if stuck in mud.
So much sky, so much ocean ...
the line between them
a dulled, quivering mirage.

And why does spring look like autumn?
Even the green is really a pale yellow,
the trees black, the air biting
every inch of bare flesh.

It's hard to be happy lately.
You mock yourself
for that last stab at love.
There wasn't even a slam of the door
as you left in the night.

Just keep driving you tell yourself.
Watch and see how you move through
time, the seasons, those frozen clouds.

Tonight the River Is a Silver Thread

Tonight the river is a silver thread,
winding its way down from the silence
of the inner hills. Does it drain the bogs?

As it crosses under the bridge,
it is full yet gentle.
The moon slides out from the cloud
and throws itself into the river.

It is then that I am
pulled out of myself
and back into the world,
into the light of the night.

Two-Legged River

Two-legged river sprawling flat
with its belly under the bridge,
with its feet kicking up boulders
into the glen, into the meadow.

The tangling and untangling
of the currents, the drunken waters
out of control but obeying
the direction of the pull.

As I move through the blue-black water,
as the crown of the sun melts my shoulders
out of their hunch of woes,
I feel the glory of summer that seems
to mean memory . . . eternity.

The Frost on the Window

The frost on the window
forms an outside pane.

In the middle of the night
the temperature rises,
the ice shatters,
and behind the shattering
flow slow streams
of freed water.

The solid pieces sway
and cling; they move
like toddlers getting
used to their limbs,
like your life moving
too fast, though it looks
and feels so slow happening.

In the room someone is singing
a song from long ago;
the words are ancient:
forsaken, slighted me, lovyer . . .
singing into the northern sky.

Before you draw the blinds
you're able to scratch your name
into the dissolving world.

What Are We Trying for Here?

What are we trying for here?

The summer is long gone,
and winter has set in
like a pack of wolves
on a bolting deer.

Sit here on this bench with me
and think it through,
here where the draft
keeps us sharp.

We are not so young;
it is easy to get tired.
Fed up.

Look there, how the sea
swallows the sun in a last
big gulp, and then already,
to our left, the moon is grinning.

If you are stretched too thin with
your worry, think again how to look
upon the frozen river, how it is moving
just the same. So look under, beyond
what the surface gives.

In on the tundra, in the bog,
far in over the hills,
so much life teeming unseen.

By some miracle,
it will all be there in the spring,
and, perhaps,
our old bones will snap to it.
Perhaps the universe will
catch us off guard,
give us grace.

So Much Light

Tired of the flatness of the city,
where all sounds run together—
the cars, the sirens, the ships' horns.
Here darkness is never black,
midnight never silent.

On a cold December day
I leave to close down
the house for the winter.
I head out along the Cape Shore road,
roll down the window to hear
the crow, the tern, the slap
of ocean on the rocks.

There is such a stillness in the old house,
a patience that seems to flood through and settle me.
I hear it, I feel it the minute I open the door.
It tells me to stay the night.

At four o'clock darkness seeps from the sky.
I go out to the shed for an armful of wood,
eat my lunch for supper, make up a bed
by the stove so I can stay close to keep the fire in.

When I go out and look up, I see
the sky is like the fire—an explosion of sparks.
The city is light years away.

In the darkness there is so much light.

Pale Winter Sky

Driving back to town,
two lanes, no guardrail,
white everywhere—
white of sky, of land,
of ptarmigan.

Only the grey rocks.
Only the movement of the car.
Only straight ahead . . . endless.

But no. The ocean
ends the sky, the ocean
ends the land. Then

an upstart streak of grey
as the dark-eyed juncos
end the white.

As I drive into the night of day.

Come Here, Listen

Come here, listen.
Along this lane shadows
lean into you.
That bun of a bird there
hovers and then
is drawn up into a shaft of air,
a current of song trailing behind him.

Here, this time of year,
the evening goes on all night.
It only stops when the blackness
smothers the light. Then lightning,
quick as a boxer's jab,
streaks the black, lights up the house.

The house is done up like a gift:
lime-green clapboard, dark-green trim.
All around, the rolling hills
roll into more green.

Inside the house sits
a button of a woman.
Beside her stands
a pole of a man.
The lightning, in a flash,
freezes them,
unlocks them as they
disappear into time.

Old Home

This is where the centuries have settled:
the oldest house in the cove.

People say it was a place of gatherings,
a place where news was traded.
Everyone has something to say about
what went on: veiled hints at wildness,
sins dressed up as badness,
badness dressed up as fun.

It was a house built for the long haul,
when winter meant
curling into someone's body heat
for the passing of kindness and love,
for the giving of it,
and the getting of it back.

Today the house holds all that
and gives it back in silence.

Root Cellar

I lift the slatted door
off the front of the cellar
and throw a light
upon a hundred years.

That great waft of time
sweeps into my face,
but the light fails to reveal
time's true depth and length.

The dust at first lies flat as
a corpse. Then it gives up
cracks of light that only add
to the mystery, slants of light that
shimmer and flicker, full of life.

There is such a softness here,
a feeling of being shown a peace
that lies everywhere unseen.

Eve of St. John the Baptist, June 23

Because the logs
are jammed with air pockets,
the fire jumps and spits.
The heave-on of rubber tires and
the insanity of kerosene
make all hell break loose—
whoops and yahoos and bottles clinked.
Victory so easily gained.

It is a pagan ritual but the pagan
has gone out of it. Still, the need to connect
to the ritual of fire lingers.
The need to look into fire.

The church stands behind us,
cozied into the glen.

Next day the remains are just that: remains.
No burnt offerings—just blackened bedsprings,
warped floor tiles, broken beer bottles.

Next week the others show up
to deal with the mess.
They cram what they can
into garbage bags.
They even out the score:
Christians 1, Pagans 1.

Coyote

The fur scant, the face sharper
than a nerve's edge.
She stands, all four legs
in a stance of fact.
There you are and here I am.

The look on her is hunger:
that's what the sagging belly says,
or too many young took her youth away.

I'm too well fed to run,
although every fibre in my body tells me to.
My fear is a quivering leaf, uncertain
where to land, and all the things that
we are told to do swirl a maelstrom
in my head.

Behind me the sunset is flaring into
the evening. I see it in her yellow eyes.
I wonder what's in her mind. I'd like
to tell her about my ordinary days,
how this meeting is extraordinary.
Even sacred. Yes, I feel that.
And I feel fear thick as bog.

Then her shoulders droop.
She turns and heads towards the barrens.

Maybe I'm a tree or
my fear smells like metal.

I follow her with my eyes
until the horizon takes her
and the fear drains out of me.

After great pain, a formal feeling comes—
Emily's poem comes floating in.

I turn to the ocean and the sinking sun,
smell the salt spray and the sweet rot of autumn,
hold for a long moment her yellow eyes in mine.

I Walk Wanting to Hear

I hear my footsteps
on the frozen path.

It has been a long winter
and spring seems shy.

But suddenly
there's the trickle of water
beneath my feet where
a brook crosses the path.

The air throws back the echo
of the crackling frost,
of the singing water,
calming the cacophony
inside my head.

After the Winter Gale

Now that the biting snarl
of the northerly has worn
itself out, I go down
to see if there's anything
left of the slipway.

Two men are in the lean-to, looking out.
Cigarette smoke trails its way
out into the flat sharpness
of the stiff air.

Frost crackles beneath my feet.

I realize the grace I am given
by this clear day: the chance to forget
the illness. It's as if the cold holds
everything tight, contained,
opens the world beyond me.

White Against White

White against white, the winter settling in,
the clouds gathering like smooth-edged glaciers.

Where the sky was once blue and grey,
now it's that confusing white of completion,
that smoky white of steam.

The mammogram found something,
not something discreet,
a definite small invasion.

And he told me this in few words,
with a deep sorrow in his face,
a sorrow that numbed me,
as if speech were the problem.

When the children were small,
I used to imagine the worst,
so there'd be no surprises,
so I wouldn't be caught off guard.
Maybe I thought that my thinking it
would shield them from disaster.

But of course if it isn't Grendel coming after you,
there's always his ugly mother waiting in the bushes.

Keeping your head above water
is a trick that takes muscle, so much coping.

A stiff upper lip was never part of our tribe,
so you let it tremble. You wonder if a year
might be enough. You inquire about tubes
and hair loss, shy to let your vanity show.

The fog moves in, a whiteout
that you can smear across the pages.
You let it obliterate words that do not
mean much anymore—after all,
there's a whole new vocabulary to learn.

The winter foghorn sounds,
it moans and groans for you
and you have to laugh.

This is still more beautiful than any life
you could have thought up.

This is what carries you away from yourself.

Like a Life Always Staring Backwards

Meanwhile, a great city is fading
in the east, and because I am facing
the wrong way, I can see it go.
—KATHLEEN GRABER

A life always staring backwards,
as if this could be undone,
that could be forgotten.

Worse are the things you thought you'd
never lose: most of your children's young
lives. The photographs only confuse you
in their tenderness. What you miss is
the touch of a tiny finger. What you have
is the great tangle of mean words, the
lost patience. But you know you are
more than that. More than then.

Because I was facing the wrong way
I got trapped in a web of fragility.
The movement took me,
the give and take loosened something,
a laugh alongside fear.

We must be watchful enough
to see it go, and return,
the great cities, the small gestures.

And So

And so then it happened:
I'm one of the many.
A shock but not a surprise;
if you get to be old enough
your chances are good.

It is a private world,
or that's the way I had to go:
no pink ribbons, no dragon boats,
but glad to know they're there.

Later a friend asks
if it makes me look at life
differently. I say it tells
me to carry on, slow down,
look up, and just breathe.

And So It Goes

My doctor doesn't care what my mother
used to call things. "Stitch": a pain in one's side.
"The Rising of the Lights": the feeling that
you're coughing up your lungs.

My doctor doesn't have time to
care about what keeps me awake at night,
she's heard it all before:
patients wondering if that "dart" or that "catch"
might be something more.

It's all breathe in, breathe out, tap-tap,
the feel for lumps, get your weight,
and out the door with you.

I ask her if maybe she's one of the O'Keefes
from across the bay, and she tells me it's Keefe,
and I say, *Yes, but you had to drop the O
during the famine in order to get the soup.*
She says, *I don't have the slightest,*
which really means *I don't give a flying fuck.*

So I left her office no wiser than when I went in.
I suppose I wanted to be distracted from the worry,
I wanted to be able to make small talk with words
that take me back to years and years ago,

to hang on to a bit of where I come from,
instead of just hanging on.

So I couldn't help myself.
On my way out I said with a wink,
So they got all of that "lumpeen," did they?

I Asked

I asked what caused it.
She said, "We don't know."
I said, "Well, everything has a cause
or more than one."
She said, "And that's it. It could be
the environment, genetics, modern love."

"Oh, of course," I said.
"That was me who swallowed
that huge lump of fool's gold called
falling in love at my age.
It had to show up somewhere."

The Air So Still

*I can feel that other day running
underneath this one . . .*
—ANNE CARSON

The air so still
        your breathing
disturbs it.

And then
        when the light leaves
the western sky
we get that last shiver
        of today.

This one day
        passing along behind us.

That Wistful Distraction

That wistful distraction of the light
as evening nudges in; it catches you,
makes you wonder if you're doing enough.

Shadows filter through the trees,
birds are in a frenzy to *Get things done*.
Ants never stop.

Your mind isn't helping.

So you pick up a novel
and read about someone else,
knowing that really
you're looking to see if
she's anything like yourself.

Meanwhile, you've lost the natural light
and on comes the solar,
world after world of light,
like fireflies pitching in the grass
and tumbling all around you.

The City. The Girl

The city is full of fog and snow,
and perhaps the fog is silently
eating the snow.

The foghorn goes on and on,
a beautiful drone we forget
is there, or that seems to be
coming from faraway.

I go to the window to watch the snow,
see instead a young woman across the street
in sweatpants and a tee-shirt,
her long, long hair hanging in streels.

She is struggling with her house key,
moving drunkenly—then she's down.
I reach out my hand,
but of course it knocks
against the window.
No! No! I say,
and my breath steams the glass.
She gets up, keeps swaying,
her head moving to some sound
that now I can almost hear.

I run across to her calling, *You okay?*
She half looks at me and says,

Iss all right, missus, iss all right.
I'm going in now. I got . . . I got this.
She gathers herself, stands at attention,
smiles hugely and falsely at me.

After a few stabs she inserts the key
and disappears inside.
I feel the snow on my bare head,
my hands.

The foghorn wails.

I stand for a moment looking.
A light comes on.
She appears at the window,
waves to me. I wave back.
It's all I know to do.

Enchanted by Yellow

It is fall and everything feels like straw,
brittle and dull.

And then a sudden glare from the sun
and the yellow grass is shot metallic yellow.
Electric yellow.

The sun slants everything,
tilting the objects in the yard,
the yellow plastic lawn chair
seems to leave the ground,
lifted by yellow and then
drops back to plain plastic yellow.

Then the shrubs on fire with it,
the dead tree alive. Me aglow,
storing the energy away for winter.

Heat Wave

In full bloom everything
thriving, fruitful, abundant,
bursting with the full of itself.

Cabbages and lilies flush, hot,
gloating in scent and colour.
Rosemary thick and leathery,
sage lapping onto the mint.

We are worn out from the heat
that prickles our skin,
sets our nerves
on high alert at nothing.

And at night we have to say,
Please, don't touch me.

Clearing Out the Shed

Clearing out the shed,
throwing out the rotten wood
light and crumbling between my fingers,
with life teeming out of it,
was something I relished doing.

Lightning-quick
repulsive earwigs
scurry.

The bloated worm plays possum,
and at the touch of my thumb
curls into a coil.
Or did I kill it?

And then you wandered into the yard
taking a simpler path at untangling
the snarl I'd gotten myself into,
and lighting a fire to burn the rest.

You came back the next day
and hauled off what didn't burn,
looked at me with eyes full of purpose.

We dove in, cleared more,
piled kelp, hauled it up the lane
for the gardens.

Later, we got tangled up
into each other's arms and legs.
Another snarl. But this one
we weren't looking to untangle.

The Sky Is Stretched Still

The sky is stretched still, pulled
tight as a grin. It is holding something,
some tender secret.

Tomorrow will be a different story:
the wind will pour in, the ocean
will echo off the hills, overtake you.
And all of it you want.

The summer is so full: it gives
and gives, an eager lover.

And you want your arms around
it all, even the thorns, that part
of love too, along with everything
the light flings at you.

This Time of the Year

This is the time of the year when
the day dies almost as soon as it begins,
and the foghorn lets you know that
it's not the moon you'll be seeing
on this night, but a white sky
cloaking your shoulders.

The air is good and clear
and calls you out into it.
The gulls have their pleading,
the starlings their gathering.
And time's song waltzes you along.

The mystery and wonder are great.
On such evenings your mind leaves
you alone so you can feel the coolness
drop on your face and hands.

And look there! Twilight winks at you
and slides under the garden gate.

After Paul Henry's Painting
Launching the Currach

In the painting all the men are back-on:
they have to be, given their task of
launching the currach.

The two men on the left are
curved into it—hauling, pushing;
the two on the right seem to be
steadying it or veering it off.

Then there is the old man
behind the veering men, who seems
to be just holding on to the boat,
not putting his thin frame into it.

He staggers.

His legs wobble. His right arm is arthritic.
His head is lowered almost in under his
rounded shoulders.

It is what's in the old man's head
that the men need:
the right time to launch, the tides,
the look of the sky.

Then he is the old man on the strand,
the cold blue-black sea to look into.
Time moving out of him and into them.

After Christopher Pratt's Painting
March at Anchor Point

I've never been there in real life,
but I know this place:
I know how the cold air hurts
as you draw it into your lungs.

Four gear sheds lined in a row
sunk in snow—
blue, grey, red, brown.
A miniature town, deserted now.
They cast shadows
from one to the other,
the child's game of imitate
what the other does.

The sky, a gothic tin sky,
with a flat ocean beneath it
doesn't give much:
the snowdrifts are the only waves.

The little light that is squeezed
from the sun is a streak of orange
bleeding into pink.

As much as the painting is of a place,
the place itself is a painting.

Things He'd Say

He liked sitting in the rocking chair.
He'd cross one leg over the other and
clasp his right elbow in his left palm,
and let his right arm point poker-stiff
in front of him, as if he was getting ready
to shake hands with anyone who came in.
There was always a lean to him, as if
relaxing into the chair might seem impolite.

That was his settled mode for talking,
for telling me what he called
Nothing at all.
As I roved out talk.
Idle talk.
Ordinary talk of people and places
he knew, and all that.

He could fill a doorway, that fellow.
This evening the flies are as thick as tobacco at a wake.
Anyone who knocks at your door after ten o'clock
in the night is nothing but a scanger.

When I served him cake on my bone china plate
he said, *That plate has a shine on it*
like a cat's eye under a bed.

Now, in the chair, there's only a ghost of him,
so when I remember things he'd say,
I whisper them into the air.

August Breezes

The wind in the grass is silent.
Flowers tremble like gentle
movements in the bath.
The spruce trees are brooding,
almost whispering.
How can so much silence be so loud?

I know what all this means:
the end of August and something
down south is heading for us,
barrelling its way up the coastline.

The swallows are gathering.
The vixen is curled in her den.
They know what's on the go.

So I flipped over the lawn chairs,
upsidedowned the picnic table,
as if to say, *The wind can't
toss them now.*

Too bad we can't flatten the roofs,
squash them to the ground
and then open them again when it passes.

The old accordion trick.

Peonies

Like juvenile ballerinas
reaching for that perfect arc
they stretch almost beyond their
spindly legs. They know how
much they have to give by
being patient.

Blooming, they sing at you,
their serenade more aubade
than nocturne. Before they
fully open they are so top heavy
that you wonder at the thought
behind the stalk they hang from.

When fully open, they look at you
every morning as if to say,
See we knew we'd make it.

All sisters gathered together
in ballroom gowns, swaying lightly.
Such an immensely happy family.

The sun must be their prince.

Daffodils

Their leaning makes me nervous:
they're like a drunk who almost falls,
and a bunch looks like it could
gang up on you. In legion.
Or they can look like a choir,
as it sings through the corona,
trumpeting that "He Has Risen."

Cocky, too. Because they have
poison—the lycorine.
But they are also Hope.

No scent? What? Is fresh not a scent?

They think they're upper class.

And look!
Battered by a cold spring,
see how they shake off
the slushy snow, come through
with that full-faced,
self-satisfied smile.

Bristly Oxtongue

You have the ugliest leaves,
pockmarked as a teenage boy,
all pimply glands that flatten out
to the ground like some sort of blob
that fell to earth and splattered.

But then you spring forth the prettiest
buttons of yellow. Up they shoot, trying
to get away from your blistering green,
a whole class of them like healthy,
bright-eyed students on the first day of school,
or very pretty maidens married off
to a hideously ugly old man.

I should pluck them away from you,
polygamous gangster! Mean ol' bastard
hoarding the belles of the county.

The belles, though, are above it all.
They've nothing to do with the ground.

They're already the sun.

Black Slug

Crawling up from
the depths of Hades.

Crawling up my drainpipe
overnight to lie there
in the sink, as though
dropped from the ceiling.

Sliming its way over
my wicker chair,
leaving a goo that
maps its journey.

Inching its way up the lane,
over rocks, over everything
in its way.

The other night I dreamed
I had one on a lead,
and Oh, I dared to follow!

So Alive

Morning

It is the crow stepping
it out on the roof that
startles us into another day.

Afternoon

So sharp and too bright,
the sun. But we want
to burn, to live our lives
so alive.

Evening

And then, at seven,
feel the warmth,
the flush under our skin,
as evening begins.

Night

It's the stars we fall for,
up all night gazing,
as they fall for us.

The Air All Around Me

The air all around me
is like a tern's shriek,
shattering through my ears.

One foot moves the other
along over the ice;
I make it music,
a low hum over the crystal bog.

Where are all the wildflowers?
The eyebright, the coltsfoot?
Do they die and resurrect?
Are they asleep
under frost and cement?

And now the wind
has gone to sing
through the telephone lines:
I hear you singing in the wire,
I can hear you through the whine.

Then the night drops
its heap of coals
from the sky.

In the Evening Light

In the evening light,
in the pale blue of sky,
last night's moon
looks over at me
from across the meadow.

I can hold her cupped in my right hand
(as I did your face two nights ago).
I know she is the moon of summer,
the shy one here, far north.
She won't show her full self
for a few days yet,
keeping secret all she knows
about the season's weather.

So high up!
We know she knows all.
The things she knows!
The devastation, the waste.
The beauty of the earth.

She knows of hearts pounding.
Look!
Her waxing encourages.
She guides the lost,
the unaligned, the seekers.
A smile? Yes, and tears
and mad abandon.

She takes us in.
She lays us down.
Whispers something we hope to hear,
something we keep yearning for.

The Evening

The evening is sinking underground,
tucking into the plush of day.

The leftovers splay across the sky—
a web of trailing night-ribbons.

Everything must rest.

The birds are singing
their last love songs of the evening:
Come away with me into the trees,
my love. Come away with me,
fold your wings, come lie with me.

Everything must rest.

As Dusk Settles

As dusk settles
into particles
of suspended light,
the chickadees flit
about, letting go of the day.

They soar, dive, cavort.
Are they fidgety? They make
the eyes blur, the tongue
silent by their chatter.

Do they take an hour
to settle in?
Is that laughter
as they toss daylight
from the bushes?

Like young lovers
giddy with delight in each other,
they tussle.

And then . . . a calm.
All the birds settle now
into ready branches,
tucking into sleep.

Evening gathering them in.

How Distinct Everything Is

How distinct everything is
in the near dark:

the spaces between
the heavy boughs

the sharpness
of the spring air

the cold cutting
vibration of the snipe
that is wearing itself out
morning and night
circling the sky.

My eyes
blindly follow my ears.

Never once have I seen it
as it cuts a trail of sound
in over the barrens,
echoing.

Or is that the trail of another sound?
My solitude echoing back at me.

The Seasons Flush the Trees

Across the lane,
evening flushes the trees,
throws golden light
from a summer girl.
Birdsongs are the laughter
she flings away,

         away,

            away!

Autumn, why so serious?
Your light slanting
like a stern mathematician
who has figured out disaster.

Dead, dead of winter.
But oh the smells of life and heat
coming from our quilts,
our skin.

And always, always,
the air we come up for
takes our breath away.

The Silence

Your right arm is out the open window,
your head thrown back on the headrest.
It's a warm August day.

Because I am driving, I cannot look
to see if the air moves the soft down
on your arm.

Your silence tells me that you're imagining
being in over the barrens we are driving through.
That's what makes you happiest.

You'd say that being there is the real happiness.
But I'd say you should see how happy,
how tranquil, your face is now.

I say nothing. Except to myself.
That I love everything that this is
and isn't yet.

Call Me by My Name

Remember how we walked towards each other?
Meet me that way again in the burnt grass.

Wear that old coat with the goose feathers
coming out of it and drifting off into the air and the sea.

We used it as a pillow, the life
slowly seeping out of it, into us.
We could run our fingers along
the coolness of the moss that lives
on the cliffs. Why couldn't we turn
our faces to all that water, sky, and sun?

I didn't know we'd never be there again.

Fool, fool, I know I am.
Was then. Still am.
But call me by my name again.

Ocean

I want the savagery of it all,
the constant heave, the stir-up,
the smash against the rocks.

Yes, I imagine myself down in it.
A little thrashing about,
but not drowning.

No, I'm not doing away with myself.

It's something else I'm after—
the freedom of dive, of flight,
the ocean's surging buoyancy.
I want to cleanse myself in its salt and ice,
in its wild, buffeting whitecaps.

And then to see, in the distance,
the beckoning, jumbled shore,
and to pull myself up onto
its slippery, kelp-strewn rocks.

Migration

They arrive in a steady thread,
a streak of ivory and gold.
Not a sound that I can hear,
not a wingbeat,
not a stirring of air.

But they are back.
I watch them from the doorstep,
one hand on the clothesline,
the other on my chest.

Like a small lift on a door latch
I feel the release of a tear. I feel it
from the well of my throat.

Summer is on the way.

And from South America to the Cape
they come again and again,
and, we hope, forever and forever.

Goose Pond

It is shaped like a water lily,
and in it water lilies float,
moving as in a waltz.

Underwater the choreographer
pulls at each long tuber,
moves them lazily as they're
lulled by the solemn duty of wind.

The pond is in over the barrens,
where the wind moves like a messenger
with secrets for news.

I watch the geese fly to the island
in the pond. It is safe there to have
their young, away from the fox
and the slinking weasel.

In the afternoon hush their sound is gentle.
They are high up and sound so far away.

The tender moss, soft as eiderdown,
smells of partridgeberries and
my sunburnt skin.
It is easy to sink, easy to let go,
so before the long walk out,
I lie down,
fall into a deep sleep.

The Neighbours Let the Grass Grow

The neighbours let the grass grow until it turned to seed.
There was a grouse in it and she came bouncing at me.
I could hear the tiny chirping of her young in the tangle.
The bouncing looked silly. How can a bounce scare anyone?
But I turned away to give her comfort.

Did I fall asleep in the chair?
Did a cat get tangled up in the grass?
Or was the mewling sex?
Cat sex, animal sex?
Not quite human. But close.

Then did I doze again?

The wind took the storm door—
crack and swoosh. I saw it sail away.
On board were rodents running in circles,
potted plants teetering, slugs sucked onto the wood,
and that sound again—the fornicating cats.

And also:

Sometimes at night there are flat dull sounds
with weight to them. A horse scratching himself
against the clapboard. A car door closing.

I don't mind not knowing what is what.
I was reared on fairy tales, tales of fairies,
tales of strange occurrences.
There's a great comfort there.

I Walk On a Thousand Small
Things a Day

At my feet a continent of moss,
dried earth and a flat stone.

I stare at what I pretend is
the edge of a stretch of land.

I am a giant looking down
at the tops of tuckamore,
of moss inlay over the coastline.

For that moment I am transported there,
like a silent drone hovering.

I bend down and rub my fingers
over the springy moss, the prickly lichen,
feeling so tender towards their smallness,
their vulnerability here on this
crowded walkway around the lake.

Everything so perfect, so small,
so easily crushed.

So open to the world.

Arabesque Lantern

It is a good size and shaped like an acorn.
White, the white of limed fences in summer.

It can house a large candle,
change itself into a flickering night sky,
its movement conjuring Shahram Nazeri
singing Rumi's poems, his soaring voice
sweeping the audience into waves of ecstasy.

And tonight his voice
makes my Arabesque flame quiver,
turns the wall into a thousand and one nights.

Tain/Táin Bó Cúailnge

In the corners of the old mirror
the tinfoil is corroding,
behind the glass
the tain is crinkling.

It takes awhile to find myself,
and when I do I'm blurry.
I look like I was born long ago,
as if two past centuries found me.

I am familiar to myself in these mirrors.
There are ghosts in the tain cracks
that say: keep on with it—
the old connection, the epics,
the cycles, the language.
They say: You've the tain to answer to.

(The *Táin Bó Cúailnge* or *The Cattle Raid of Cooley* is an epic in
Irish mythology.)

Seisiún

There comes an age
when you'd think
that all the sentiment
would have run out of you,
or that use would
wear it thin.

I do not understand
the longing that
the *sean nós*
pulls out of me,
as if an ancient voice
has a hold to
a thread in my chest
and every now and then
gives it a good tug
at a word, a sound . . .
a memory.

And it isn't me remembering.
And I don't know that ghost's name.

Seaweed On a Winter Beach

My daughter and I climbed up the seaweed,
mound after mound of pile-up.
It was the middle of winter and February storms
tore the kelp from the guts of the ocean,
and the waves grabbed it,
hove it up onto the sand.

Day after day after day the waves
kept heaving and heaving.
We climbed up and we slid down,
we climbed up another pile and down.

We were sea nymphs on dry land
claiming our kelp-hair,
our kelp-clothes.
We gulped the air into our lungs
and felt the grit of salt and sand.

We climbed and collapsed on pile after pile,
we stretched our limbs out to the frost
and snow. We stayed until the burning
of the cold set in.
Until our sodden clothes threatened
to freeze us in place.

Sea Foam

The wind is off the water
and is pushing the waves
in a frenzy to the sand.
It is a ruckus of jump
and hiss and chase.

Like children's blown bubbles,
the sea foam blows onto the sand
and into the grass.

It tumbles into the beach pea,
the sea thrift, the oyster leaf.
And rests.
Clings.

A soft downy brown
frothing and bubbling,
coming together
into one new thing.

And it travels farther in
than the sea ever will.

Sounds at Night

Things do go bump
in the night:
a dull faraway thud
of something shifting,
or something dropped.

It is what the sea
does with rocks:
a haul and pull,
a sound like
nervous swallowing.

A letting go, the hollow
after-sound of sound.

At Night the Sea

*It came to me then that the sea
is not a pattern, it is a struggle.*
—COLM TÓIBÍN

At night the sea frightens me,
the moon its only mistress,
and the moon only smiles,
sly and slanting,
carefree and faraway.

The ocean is as mad as the wind.
Even from the comfort of the sand
I sense its raw energy.

It is all push and pull,
all force, all solitude and sprawl.
But utterly contained.
Nothing to do with us,
yet its pull owns us.

To be alone with the sea at night
is a kind of surrender, or
a communion with eternity.

Something so deep
must hold such darkness.

The Wind Has Robbed the Legs Off a Madwoman

> *When they want to know what we*
> *were like they will search for the*
> *barriers we raised against the wind.*
> —DERMOT HEALY

The wind has robbed the legs off a madwoman,
and her skirts are flung out into the spheres.

All the birds have wintered out. There are only
slants of light that dance along with the madwoman:

the old bone dance.

Our limbs are tucked up in under the wintering sky.
We say we'll dance come spring, come thaw, come love.

The wood builds up the fire to a frightening flare,
but still it is colder inside than out.

After two days the flies wake up. They are so slow.
Not at all happy. Not even hungry.

All around the house the crazy woman carries on.
What music does she hear? The heavenly bodies?

Or is there a madder music somewhere
that undoes us all?

Acknowledgements

ArtsNL

City of St. John's

Writers' Trust of Canada

Ed Kavanagh, an incredible editor — *Go raibh míle maith agat.*

A variation of the poem "Two-Legged River" was commissioned by Kelly Walsh for Lady Cove Women's Choir.

Poet and playwright AGNES WALSH was born in Placentia, Newfoundland. She has published three previous collections of poetry: *In the Old Country of My Heart* (Killick Press, 1996), *Going Around with Bachelors* (Brick Books, 2007), and *Oderin* (Pedlar Press, 2018). Her work as founder, artistic director, and writer for the Tramore Theatre Troupe (1999–2012) won her the Newfoundland and Labrador Hospitality Award. In 2011, her collection of plays *Answer Me Home* was published by Breakwater Books. She was the inaugural poet laureate for the City of St. John's from 2006 to 2009 and was awarded the 2020 Hall of Honour Award from ArtsNL.